EVERYTHING A WOMAN CAN'T DO

KEVIN ROWE

CONTENTS

ACKNOWLEDGEMENTS

Writing requires support and inspiration. For this book, devoted thanks go out to:

God

Kathy Rowe, my wife*my Peach

Dr. James T. Reese

Sandy Reese

Pearl Rowe

Pearline Mosley

Richard Runkle

I would also like to thank all the women of the world and all of the amazing women that have touched, challenged, and enriched my life. You were instrumental in the growth of my wisdom, passion, and compassion.

REFLECTIONS ONE...

Do you know what it is?...

?... What is it...?
?...

REFLECTIONS TWO...

Do you feel you know?...

?... What is it...?
?...

REFLECTIONS THREE...

Do you think you know?...

?... What is it...?
?...

REFLECTIONS FOUR...

Some thoughts you have may be true...

?... What is it...?
?...

REFLECTIONS FIVE...

Do you really know?...

?... What is it...?
?...

ELUCIDATION

L et me begin all that we are to explore together by introducing thought upon an intriguing subject that captivates my interest. I have been enamored with it for many years and I have rendered many years of study to it. The subject that I speak of is a flower, so innocent and delicate, but has the power through its beauty to impart a unique form of pleasure into the heart of mankind. Because of this, that flower has the uncommon potential to give morsels of joy to masses of people on a daily basis.

It is good to be around people who have joy and make it a point to spread it to others. One can get caught up in the residuals of happiness as well while being around the joyful people. This is a good thing. We can all use regular doses of beauty and pleasure because these are the very things that seem to be needed most and lacking the most in the hearts of people today. Examining the characteristics of a flower right now may seem a bit trivial to you and that is okay. I understand. Wisdom only comes to a person when wisdom comes to a person. It is then up to that person to receive wisdom as it awaits. Are you ready to receive?

Through the unique joy that a flower imparts to a heart, even for short stolen moments of time, that flower has exhibited its command of influence. It has exhibited its power to affect positive change in people. If this is true, it can be said that a flower has the power to enhance joy within people. So, if that flower can enhance or induce joy within people, it has the potential to use that same joy process to begin influencing the hearts of nations of people. In doing so, that flower effectively advances its momentum toward improving the hearts of an entire civilization of people by inducing internal pleasure from the beauty of said flower.

How so, your mind may now ask? My response to this question... THAT FLOWER...is the flower of radiant color with amazing beauty that captivates the eyes and momentarily paralyzes the mind with awe. Such a flower commands focus upon the most intricate detail that only penetrates the mind's eye imbued with love, which is the origin of the creation. It is then revealed to the heart - the great joy in witnessing and beholding the untampered beauty of love. The mere essence of the definition of a flower symbolizes pure simplistics of love. And the amazing thing about that flower is that from that flower, you receive the pollination that is necessary to help create an atmosphere of optimism based upon the beauty that is witnessed from observing that same flower. And sometime after pollination, time will follow time long enough to nurture the growth and spread of more flowers.

With the proliferation of the spreading of such flowers of beauty, we progress further in improving and beautifying our world. It is evident to me that flowers are needed to bring joy, to bring clarity, to bring beauty, to bring benefit to the heart's mind, to bring benefit to the eye's heart, to bring benefit to the human being to become better. You see, becoming better should be a personal goal of every human. I believe it should be one of the main goals of humanity and of human life. I believe properly nourished flowers have the ability to maintain their individual innocence and individuality. I also believe that a flower maintains its strength because its strength lies within love and love is the greatest power on this earth. And love is the only thing that can conquer evil and hatred.

THAT FLOWER...is where the pedals are of different colors and of different shapes. THAT FLOWER, is without preconceived notions about anything except being all that it is and all that it is, is being one form of truth.   THAT FLOWER, speaks not with a voice but resounds throughout the universe. THAT FLOWER, is so unique that it doesn't look exactly like any other even though they are extraordinarily similar. It even has its own DNA - that DNA that distinguishes it from the next - that next pedal, that next stem. THAT FLOWER, can be a gateway to peace.

THAT FLOWER can be handed to the heart of an enemy and transform him into a friend. You see, the mind is in control of the body and the body is servant to the mind. So, if THAT FLOWER is specifically given to change the heart of an enemy by making him a friend, and actually does so, then THAT FLOWER confirms the power that I speak of. THAT FLOWER, accomplishes these things because it has the awesome ability to influence attitudes located inside the mind's mindset.

THAT FLOWER, Oh, THAT FLOWER – is that special something given that lives on because it has been destined to do so.   THAT FLOWER, is one of the greatest gifts ever given to mankind. THAT FLOWER, is every girl that is born into the world. THAT FLOWER, is every woman that walks this earth that gives birth to every child. THAT FLOWER, is inside the heart of every man that is good and even bad. THAT FLOWER, is part of the basis and foundations of peace. THAT FLOWER, is also the ingredient that is requisite inside of hope.

THAT FLOWER, can bring a smile in the midst of crying tears. THAT FLOWER, can begin to heal any heart that has been crushed or psychologically carved into many pieces. THAT FLOWER, can comfort a soul even in the midst of sympathy or in the midst of personal trial and tribulation. THAT FLOWER, can be a jolt of encouragement during a serene walk with terminal illness. THAT FLOWER, has its importance because it never changes unless it is made to change by the hands of the heart of man.

THAT FLOWER, in its original state, is all that I have said it is, and even more. THAT FLOWER, is the vessel that enhances love. THAT FLOWER, stands as a symbol of greatness. THAT FLOWER, stands as a symbol of sensitivity. THAT FLOWER, stands as a symbol of unity. THAT FLOWER, is LOVE. THAT MAGNIFICENT FLOWER is A WOMAN!

WOMAN

In this life there are many wonders that leave the mind of man in awe. When I say wonders, I am casually referring to what is commonly known as "Wonders of the World." I am referring to wonders that find their way into any field of thought and remain absent of explanation. These wonders can originate from any field of personal interest that produce unexplained occurrences. Wonders can also occur within all regions of the world as well as within any galaxy above us. In fact, wonders can exist exclusively as self-imposed fiction created from the imagination of man.

Most wonders of the world remain without explanation indefinitely – until genius falls upon the mind of man and provide the tools of adequate explanation. Similarly, in this life within this world, there are enormous possibilities. Anything is possible! Possibilities in the rawest sense of definition are simply potentialities without the consideration of aptitude. Similarly, we also find within this world something called impossibilities. Impossibilities are those things in life that cannot be done.

Who is she? She was never made to be invisible, ignorant, or psychologically mute. To the contrary, she was made to be wise, beautiful, strong, creative, cultivating, captivating, and stimulating. She's a...

    daughter

    sister

mother

muse

leader

lover

life-giver

teacher

She's a timeless Goddess worthy of respect, that thing that subjectively commands of her augmented self-respect. This respect comes from the deep rivers of her soul. She is here, this beautiful flower, to pollinate the earth with beauty. She's here to selflessly cultivate and replenish the psychophysiological storehouse of mankind. She is here to be herself for the entire world to experience, to feel, and to see. She is woman and all that it is. And all that it is – is she. A woman's true nature is to be like a chameleon, having the unique ability to adapt to any situation to achieve any goal. All she asks is to be given what she is often without – equal opportunity. She can be and achieve any and everything her splendid mind decides to receive, believe, and achieve! This fact is often overlooked, understated, or discarded by men for reasons left to be unknown. She is the ultimate riddle that no man can claim to solve. She is a beautiful vessel of multiplicity able to penetrate the mind's soul and leave behind contagious, unmitigated desire. Yet, without remorse, this beautiful being is often treated as if she is of secondary importance.

This leads me to ask an important question. Why must a woman continue to fight to be respected in the home, in the workplace, and in the world? Time within history shall remain the recorder of man-made choices noting the insufficient prioritization of relevant protections for the understated rights of women. It shall also record all missed opportunities of man to protect and elevate her human capital. How long must the vision of man remain unfit when the eyes of his mind look upon the value of a woman? This same vision has no problem acquiring clarity when looking upon himself and upon all others alike.

Imagine, if you will, living within a prism whose rays fall just short of their intended target depriving said life of proper illumination. Imagine living within a life that has been subliminally devaluated in the minds of a society in which it permanently resides. History speaks of those guilty of facilitating the latter and it also speaks to those who still do. Imagine that? Unfortunately, these are the intangibles a woman receives when smiled upon by the ugly face of all discrimination. It shall never be right to make any human feel of lesser value. Moreover, it shall never be right to selectively minimize the raw and often untapped potential of any person - not now, not later, not ever! Everybody is somebody! I emphatically repeat for your heart, "Everybody is Somebody!" This also means "Every Somebody can never be a Nobody!" For these very reasons, no one should ever contemplate treating any "Somebody" as a "Nobody". *If the mindsets of people would honor these simple facts, all discrimination would fall quickly upon its deaf bed.* We must raise our benevolent consciousness to bravely lean our understanding and actions toward true equality - an equality that sees, feels, speaks, and lives unmitigated equal. Hearts must be taught. Mindsets must be adjusted. Behavior must be modified. If this happens, all forms of discrimination would then take up permanent residency in the eternal vault of forbidden afterthought.

WHAT SHE OFFERS

A woman exists as the vessel specifically designed to save mankind from extinction. History is the long story of this fact and history shall remain the sole arbiter of all related questions and challenges to this claim.

The blessings from her heart, a Woman's heart...have nourished and encouraged unspeakable numbers of lives via kind words and actions of emotional warmth. Just look back on your life for a moment and reflect on a special time when a woman (mother, aunt, grandmother, sister, friend, or acquaintance) comforted you when your emotions and/or body were challenged or damaged in some way. It was a time when you were unsure of what to do or what to say. It was a time when a woman voluntarily stepped in and out of pure concern for your well-being, she provided what was necessary to help you and protect you.

I have learned that the basic function of the heart is to pump needed blood throughout our body to transport oxygen and nutrients to respective organs. Also, this same heart acts as an emotional command center for our mind to respond to effectively. I believe the heart to be especially important to us because it is the special reservoir specifically designed and designated to house the most powerful force on this planet – LOVE. You see, Love is so powerful that it exists as the only force capable of destroying hate. Love is that force every woman has plenty of. Love is what makes her heart powerful, yet tender and sensitive to even the most subtle touches of inspiration. The blessings of the heart of a woman have even been the reason why war has waited when all reason had been vacated. Presidents, leaders, and Kings alike have benefited from some form of support from a woman. A woman is so unique that she can have a bad that's so good and a good that's so bad at the same time and still field meals, assignments, advice, and affections effectively. She has the unique ability to subliminally and psychologically speak within all levels of greatness which is divinely driven by the sweet essence of her soul. Yes, I repeat, war has waited when all reason was vacated… What a source of power! A Woman! What a beautiful being!

The blessings from her hands, a Woman's hands…have physically held the bodies of domestic violence, the bodies of women wounded from the intense pain of breakup, the bodies of child abuse, and the bodies of rape and incest. The hands of a woman are often soiled from the same and even damaged from the constant lifting of pain, filth, and trash left upon others by others. A woman, at times, finds herself having to decide whether to care enough to dare herself enough to act. A woman is divinely endowed with spiritual might. Each day doubt may visit her and try to impart its unwanted influence upon her. But each day, she has to mentally overpower its power to believe in belief because belief is her hope's because. Yes, the hands of a woman may often get soiled or bruised, all while supporting some form of need. But when it's showtime, she can flip the scrip, dip her hips, and ready any ship! She's a Woman!

The blessings from her body, a Woman's body…has satisfied the needs of mankind since the time of eve. So soft, so silky, so complete, with intangible tantalizations of her eyes of euphoric aura and the salacious design of her unique physique, this masterpiece of mortal art is a tangible Goddess divinely endowed with love. Every single day she adorns her body to solicit appeal from the conscious subconsciousness of a man's desire. This exists as an everyday blessing to all of him. This heavenly blessed physique boasts diverse individuality complimenting a specifically tailored personality. How splendid is it for man to receive the psychological gift of witnessing imaginations believed from her body. Dear Goddess of love as you read, stop now and take a bow, I salute your beautiful body! She's a Woman!

The blessings from her mind, a Woman's mind…possesses deceptive strength and it has significantly enhanced the potential of all greatness starting from her first glance into a baby's eyes. This mental strength is governed somehow by 100 billion neurons active inside the walls of her extraordinary brain which are harmoniously connected to 37 trillion cells permeating throughout her body heavenly infused with love. It is the love of a mother (a woman) that first introduces love to a baby. This is done by igniting love's lasting effect upon said child by the gentile touch and whispers rendered from the heart of that mother into the sweet soul of a child. There is much work to be done in the process of developing the mind and natural potential of a child. Every good mother spends innumerable seconds, minutes, hours, days, contemplating the progress, safety, physical development, and mental nutrition of her child or a child she is committed to care for. There are no academic degrees bestowed upon dedicated women for motherhood other than degrees of unconditional love that are acquired through the sweat equity of devoted trial and error.

Be careful not to overlook the mental excellence rendered by a good mother – a woman. The blessing of the mind of a woman has been experienced by nearly every human that walks upon this earth. That is a fact! Additionally, it is important to note that the brilliance of a woman's mind has shown no boundaries. The brilliance of a woman's mind has touched and even transformed many industries of the world. The human brain is one of the most powerful organs within the human body and it is capable of directing that same body to do amazing things. Just as with man, the woman's brain also has the phenomenal ability to create with excellence, motivate with excellence, and lead with excellence.

She's a Woman!

A "GLIMPSE"

The history of America is saturated with women pioneers who fought for their human rights and made enormous strides in the fields of politics, science, sports, art, and literature. During the Victorian Era of the 1800's, a man's basic concern centered around success and moving up the social ladder. He was extremely competitive and devoted all of his time and energy toward his work. A woman, on the other hand, was basically concerned with meeting the Victorian Era's popular standard of being the virtuous woman. As such, she was expected to uphold and honor four characteristics of the virtuous woman which were piety, purity, submissiveness, and domesticity. Was this good for the woman? Was this healthy for her self-esteem? Did this encourage her to be free to explore other talents and interests? I find these questions to be easy to answer if approaching them from the experience and freedoms of today's woman. However, during the Victorian Era it appeared that women's opinions regarding self and life were of less importance. The only thing that mattered then was that she knew her place and never deviate from it if she wanted to be married and provided for. It was expected of her to cook, to clean, and to take care of any other things necessary within the home. It was the woman's duty to ensure that the home was orderly and peaceful in return for her husband's financial security, protection, and social status. During this period, a woman received reverence from her husband as well as society as long as her domestic responsibilities were performed flawlessly without error. Things had to change and they did change because she deemed it so!

Dear lady of love just in case your ears have never heard the voices of your triumph song, I have written the lyrics of your special love song below for your eyes to see and your heart to hear…

NOTHING CAN STOP YOU! NOTHING SHALL EVER STOP YOU! YOU ARE WOMAN!!!

The lyric sound something like this…

- 1778~Deborah Sampson disguised herself as a man and fought in the American Revolution
- 1849~Elizabeth Blackwell became the first US woman to earn a medical degree
- 1854~Florence Nightingale introduced nursing innovations in Britain
- 1881~Clara Barton founded the American Red Cross
- 1898~Julia Morgan became first woman admitted to the Ecole de Beaux-Arts in Paris (best architecture school in the world – and later became the first woman licensed as an architect in California)
- 1903~Marie Curie became the first woman to receive Nobel Prize for her work on radioactivity
- 1916~Margaret Sanger opened the first birth control clinic in the United States
- 1921~Edith Wharton became the first woman to win a Pulitzer Prize
- 1923~Activist Alice Paul proposed the Equal Rights Amendment
- 1924~Nellie Toyloe Ross became the first female governor
- 1928~Amelia Earhart became the first woman to fly an airplane across the Atlantic
- 1933~Frances Perkins became President Franklin D. Roosevelt's Secretary of Labor, the first female member

of a Presidential cabinet

- 1955~Seamstress Rosa Parks refused to give up her bus seat to a white passenger in Montgomery, Alabama and became a civil rights pioneer
- 1961~Katherine Johnson, an African-American space scientist and mathematician, calculated key trajectories for Alan Shepard - the first American Astronaut to travel in space
- 1966~Betty Goldstein Friedan founded the National Organization for Women (NOW)
- 1972~Katharine Graham became the first woman to become CEO of a Fortune 500 Company
- 1974~Isabel Martínez de Perón became the President of Argentina and the first female president in the world
- 1975~Sharon Crews became the first female African American weather anchor on television
- 1976~Barbara Walters became the first female nightly network news anchor
- 1977~Janet Guthrie became the first woman to drive in the Indy 500
- 1978~Mary Clarke became the first woman promoted to Major General in the U.S. Army
- 1979~Susan B. Anthony became the first woman honored on a U.S. coin
- 1981~President Ronald Reagan nominated Sandra Day O'Connor to be the first woman on the Supreme Court - she was confirmed and appointed
- 1982~Alice Walker became the first black woman to win the Pulitzer Prize for fiction
- 1983~Sally Ride became the first woman in space by flying on the Space Shuttle Challenger
- 1984~Joan Benoit won the first women's Olympic Marathon

- 1985~Penny Harrington became the first female Police Chief of a major U.S. city; Portland PD
- 1986~Ann Bancroft became the first woman to complete a trek to the North Pole
- 1987~Aretha Franklin became the first woman elected to the Rock and Roll Hall of Fame
- 1988~Shawna Robinson became the first woman to win a NASCAR-sanctioned race
- 1989~Ileana Ros-Lehtinen became the first Hispanic woman elected to Congress
- 1990~Antonia Novello became the first female U.S. Surgeon General
- 1991~Geraldine Morrow became the first female President of the American Dental Association
- 1992~Manon Rheaume became the first woman to play in an NHL game
- 1992~Carol Moseley Braun became the first black woman elected to the U.S. Senate
- 1993~Janet Reno became the first female Attorney General of the United States.
- 1994~The Church of England ordained its first female priests
- 1995~Roberta Cooper Ramo became the first female President of the American Bar Association
- 1997~Madeleine Albright became the first female Secretary of State
- 1998~Julie Taymor became the first woman to win the Tony Award for Best Director
- 1999~Nancy Ruth Mace became the first woman to graduate from The Citadel
- 2000~Kathleen A. McGrath became the first woman to command a U.S. Navy warship

- 2001~Gale A. Norton became the first female Secretary of the Interior and Secretary of Agriculture in U.S. history
- 2002~Halle Berry became the first black woman to win the Academy Award for Best Actress
- 2003~Shirin Ebadi became the first Muslim woman to win the Nobel Peace Prize
- 2004~Catherine Pepinster became the first woman to be Editor in Chief of The Tablet Magazine
- 2005~Condoleezza Rice became the first black woman to serve as U.S. Secretary of State
- 2006~Michelle Bachelet became the first female President of Chile
- 2007~Nancy Pelosi became the first woman to serve as Speaker of the US House of Representatives - making her the highest-ranking woman in US government history
- 2009~Nancy Lieberman became the first female head coach of an NBA-affiliated team
- 2010~Kathryn Bigelow became the first woman to win an Oscar for Best Director
- 2013~Mary Barra became the first female chief executive officer of General Motors
- 2015~Sarah Thomas became the first woman to referee for the NFL
- 2016~Hillary Clinton became the first female presidential nominee of a major party
- 2020~Katie Sowers became the first woman and first openly gay coach in Super Bowl history
- 2021~Kamala Harris became first female, first Black and first South-Asian Vice President in U.S. history

"IMPOSSIBLE" ...

What does impossible mean to a woman? Allow me a few moments within time to briefly examine this most relevant question of analysis? Merriam-Webster defines the word impossible as "incapable of being or of occurring." After many years of study and observation in the laboratory of life, I have found the woman, her, she, to be extraordinarily endowed with intuition and fortitude. I absolutely love the woman for she can flawlessly bear the face of an angel, the structure of a goddess, and the grace of a queen. I humbly state what is to follow from my learned heart and mind instructed by a life touched, raised, and uniquely tuned by amazing women. You see, she, that infinite flower of power, has made S stand for Strong, H stand for Hope, and E stand for Entity (i.e., Strong Hope Entity) in the word SHE infinitely.

Just as she stands, after rising each morning, standing alone within herself, about herself, surrounded by all of her, she briefly reflects. She is gorgeous above gorgeous, poised, and ready to make her day, your day, somebody's day, amazing because she stepped into it. She can render sagacious thought to the many spontaneous complexities of life. She selflessly uses the same to make a difference in the lives of others even though the residuals are usually of some personal cost to her. Why does she continue to do for others when most won't? It is part of her personal DNA to give in give-less situations. Regarding matters of the heart, it is part of her DNA to notice even the smallest of detail and care when the same is not obvious to all involved. She is not perfect. She shall never be perfect. Nevertheless, she is still worth loving. Nevertheless, she is still worth appreciating and respecting. I repeat, Nevertheless, she is still worth loving! Nevertheless, she is still worth appreciating and respecting!

...And just when you think she is about to fall, she finds the courage from the deep caverns of her heart to sojourn just a little more, and a little more, and a little more, often without the luxury of well-intentioned help. It is simply amazing to me how a woman can find mental, physical, and spiritual pathways through her subconscious-being to love deeply in the absence of love. How is this so? Is it that she is barren of self-respect? Is it that she is depleted of pride? Is it that she is destitute of courage? I think not. I believe that based upon the many lies rendered to her discerning ears and vivacious eyes, she has developed the unique ability to adapt whatever it may be to an internal duty to goodness, grace, family, and unconditional love.

She may walk the floors of worry yet comforted by hopeful feet. She may sweep the decks of disgust yet promote optimism for improvement. She may hold all heads of sadness within her bosom yet remain ever filled with unconditional love. She may cleverly extract love from lovelessness and never murmur a word about the same. She may mount sweet pieces of peace upon the shoulders of war, yet never seek glory or personal credit. She may work for all that she desires, you desire, and we desire - devoid of fatigue, yet never miss a beat. She may secretly crave even a minute morsel of appreciation, yet often not be allowed to taste it. She often walks in the shadows of a man while simultaneously carrying his burdens along with hers and often tames herself to never speak of it. She teaches, she nurtures, she nourishes, she protects, she encourages, she loves, and she diligently cultivates the minds of her children all while simultaneously doing the same for her man.

You ask what does the word impossible mean to a woman? I

believe the word impossible makes no appearance in the mind of a woman because she simply can't afford it.

"NOW, SOMEBODY PLEASE TELL ME EVERYTHING A WOMAN CAN'T DO?..."

Before meeting the world each day, her emotions become naked before him, and he fails to notice their bareness. She thinks of creative ways to capture necessary attention from him that is worthy of her deepest unsolicited surrenders – but often to no avail. She often stands to his front partially self-exposed and guarded every moment in his presence. This same self-exposure appears whenever she falls under the welcomed power of the desire she has for his masculine voice and his suggested raw masculinity. A natural impatience finds its way to the pathway to her mind only to be halted by the powerful influence of love. Her love is strong, and it can handle bouts of neglect, envy, jealousy, and even infidelity – while gracefully being held together by the compassionate hands of hope. These hands of hope draw their strength from the pure power of her love.

Make no mistake, a woman may at times appear foolish or act foolish, but she is definitely no fool, especially when it comes to getting whatever it is that she truly wants. She will apply the best of her mind to achieve whatever she truly wants to achieve! However, success and even potential success is difficult when the standards that she must bear are doubled. More than idled words and gestures of passivity are requisite to fix this. Doing without or going without is not a self-imposed skill for her but rather attributes that have found tenure in her massive toolbox of life. We all have a toolbox of life that equips us with capabilities and solutions for the many challenges we face in life. Some are filled with positivity and yield mostly positive results, while others, unfortunately, are filled with negativity and yield mostly negative results. All of which have bearing upon society. I urge you to only seek to put positive tools in your toolbox of life because what you put in truly is what you will be pulling out to use when facing life challenges.

I have found that a woman is willing to give her heart and her body pure conviction when seeking true love. Her mind, her body, and her emotions become ultra-focused on experiencing and acquiring both the partial fantasy as well as the reality of true love. Whenever she ignites this desire, her determination finds intensity and altitude. All these things combined are amazing gifts afforded any spouse or partner. Is this not enough to qualify to be truly loved? Is this not suffice of her to render? Must the myths associated with women continue to plague her happiness? Must the many false definitions of beauty continue to plague her concern and self-worth, both in and outside of her relationships - even with that with self? I now ask you this question, "How often do you think of a woman's contribution to love?" "How often do you think of a woman's contribution to our economy?" Moreover, "How often do you think of a woman's contribution to humanity?" If "not often" is your answer, you fit comfortably within the category I entitle "most people". While this should be surprising to all, sadly it is not. I do not feel that she is asking too much in her quest to feel love, share love, to live in love and to be fully respected. In fact, she deserves this and much, much, more.

ANSWER THIS?

Why adore her?... Why not adore the smell of her true essence? Why not savor that sweet smell of her kindness exuding from the wonderful light of her eyes so precious? Why not rob the bank of guilty pleasure just one surreal moment from the safe of appreciation - just to momentarily gaze upon her - paralyzed by sweet imagination? Why not unlock the mental door to sheltered thoughts and remember sweet subliminal touches she graciously renders to all? Why not move toward her in awe of her celestial presence? Why not extend to her a portion of your internal peace? Does any of these questions strike you as being unreasonable? It seems quite evident to me that many, and even perhaps most people, never even pause for even one moment to truly consider her.

Oftentimes, unfortunately, true consideration is not even given by her to herself. Perhaps this is due to the mental footprints of some form of abuse embedded in her mind. What a brilliantly tantalizing masterpiece of strength, ingenuity, wisdom, and dual beauty - handcrafted individually by the hands of God worthy to be adored! *Why adore her?...The facts speak it best, there need not be further reasons for any mental test. She is bad! She has always been ideal! It is time for everyone, and I do mean everyone, to know and recognize that She is real! SHE IS WOMAN! Why adore her? Why adore her?... Questions still? Who ELSE can fill the bill?*

Why cherish her?... Why not cherish her, a being so worthy

of superlatives? May I impose momentarily upon your present consciousness to highlight just a few hidden truths known to me about every her, every she, every girl, and every woman? ...And it flows like this: The proverbial "man's best friend" will lick the face of a man and that man will cherish it for a lifetime. A woman, on the other hand, will caress the wounds of a man's pride and hold it, nurture it, and heal it until he is able to step into new or renewed confidence. Is that not enough for man to cherish her? A true understanding of reality will obliterate any thoughts of comparison here.

Why cherish her?... Whenever inspiration needs inspiration, who is called upon first? When emotional nutrition is warranted, yet absent, who is called upon first? When happiness and pleasure are craved in the night, in the day, and in every way, who is called upon first?...*The facts speak it best, there need not be further reasons for any mental test. She is bad! She has always been ideal! It is time for everyone, and I do mean everyone, to know and recognize that She is real! SHE IS WOMAN! Why cherish her? Why cherish her?... Questions still? Who ELSE can fill the bill?*

Why respect her?... Why not respect her? Perhaps there is relative ease exhibited within the minds of those unfamiliar with the truth about her in their attempts to minimize her. Why is this so? I believe this is the result of the routine practice of disrespect fueled by misguided ignorance. Oftentimes, this disrespect is cleverly disguised within patterns of misbehavior cloaked underneath informal norms.

Let's set the record straight, for all minds unfamiliar with the understanding that a woman deserves respect. A woman should be respected because she is worthy on all fronts of life. A woman should be respected based ultimately upon her overall value and magnificent contributions to every society. You see, because of her unique ability to give birth, she exists as the divine vessel that has saved and continues to save mankind from extinction. Why respect her?...*The facts speak it best, there need not be further reasons for any mental test. She is bad! She has always been ideal! It is time for everyone, and I do mean everyone, to know and recognize that She is real! SHE IS WOMAN! Why respect her? Why respect her?... Questions still? Who ELSE can fill the bill?*

*Why believe in her?...*Why not believe in her...She believes in believing in you. What is wrong with the wanting inside of her to desire from you confidence in her abilities and the design of her destiny? Is she not worthy of what she offers selflessly to you? Must she only be left to fantasize about a need that should be a given for her love? Goethe said **"He is dead in this world who has no belief in another."** What more must a woman do to be deserving of a man's confidence in her? Does he expect her to beg for his trust in her word? Must she bury the pain of his disbelief deep within her while maintaining belief in him? Failing to believe in a woman, your woman, is essentially failing to believe in her virtue as a woman. You see, integrity is a virtue. Keep walking away satisfied while dismissing this need, and you will find your deficient love permanently dismissed. She was a Goddess when her love met you. She remains that flower of love today. Real men can recognize this supreme quality easily. What now does this say about the man you claim to be? A virtuous woman is ever worthy of your belief!...*The facts speak it best, there need not be further reasons for any mental test. She is bad! She has always been ideal! It is time for everyone, and I do mean everyone, to know and recognize that She is real! SHE IS WOMAN! Why believe in her? Why believe in her?... Questions still? Who ELSE can fill the bill?*

Why love her?...   Why not love her? Why not love a wonderful being uniquely endowed with ubiquitous appeal and sensuality? Why not love the love that she gives freely from the depths of the soul of her soul? If you have never loved or been in love before, you may not understand how and why this is important and relevant. But for those of you who have been loved before and have been in love before, you should understand this about love. Love sweetens the bitter tastes of life. Love reinforces the heart's walls of security. Love bonds the often-fragile fabric of relationships. Love upholds the best of good. Love, true love, always begins from within. A woman is all that I have described because she is what she is – a WOMAN. There is no other creature on earth that equally compares to a woman. There is no other creature on earth that can give birth to a human child. There is no other creature on this earth that has the unique power to influence-influence itself, and make it desire even unwanted actions or events.

When man looks for desirability of himself, who does he call or seek first? A Woman! When man seeks to feel all of the complete emotions from achieving personal success, who does he call or seek first? A Woman! When a man seeks to influence and persuade the minds of others, indicating a sense of grandeur, stability, and/or credibility, who does he call first? A Woman! Again, I state with truth, A woman's nature is to be like a chameleon, able to adapt to any situation. Be careful not to abuse the greatest gift that she has to gift to you. For it is that same gift that shall ever bless you when you heart is ever devoid of joy, your mind is robbed of confidence, and your wealth or supposed good fortune evaporates into thin air. It is that special gift, the love of a Woman, that will stand undaunted and fill, encourage, and heal all that which has been devoided, robbed, and evaporated...*The facts speak it best, there need not be further reasons for any mental test. She is bad! She has always been ideal! It is time for everyone, and I do mean everyone, to know and recognize that She is real! SHE IS WOMAN! Why love her? Why love her?... Questions still? Who ELSE can fill the bill?*

"NOW, SOMEBODY PLEASE TELL ME EVERYTHING A WOMAN CAN'T DO?"

TRUTH UNIMAGINED

There is one thing that a woman can't do…but everything else is fair game! Here's one thing that a woman just can't do - "A WOMAN CAN NEVER BE INVALID!"

There are many misconceptions prevalent today about the capabilities and contributions of the woman. Some expound that the woman is incapable of effective leadership, which is grossly untrue. Others proport the reasoning for such a claim is due to the woman being too emotional, which bears no truth as well. I will halt my listing of such rhetoric here because I find your time to be too valuable to be wasted on noting insignificant hyperbole.

One of the reasons a woman can never be invalid is that she helps to preserve cultures. It is the woman who is typically one of the chief preservationists of culture and tradition for most cultures. She is normally one of the people who masters, preserves, protects, and teaches treasured recipes and tradition. This makes her valid and substantiates her validity.

When reflecting upon social activism, who comes to mind first? Who is it that is more involved in social activism in the schools? Answer: Women. Who is it that is more involved in social activism in the communities? Answer: Women. Who is it that is more involved in social activism in the workplace? Answer: Women. Who is it that is more involved in social activism in local political campaigns? Answer: Women. For these few reasons alone, women are too active and too important to social activism to ever be invalid.

It has been proven that men are basically a visual creature. Men often marry women based largely upon physical/visual attraction. I am not saying this is right nor am I implying that all men choose their spouses in this manner. The point I seek to make here is that women remain an object of beauty to man today. For example, look at the role the woman plays in the reality of man's success. I guess you can call her a silent partner in a significant number of all male success stories. She may not be officially named nor recognized publicly, but somehow, she played a part. It is the woman who feeds the body of man while motivating and stroking his ego whenever needed. It is the woman that elevates his pride with her beauty and representation of him or family during all social gatherings. It is the woman who meets all the stated and unstated needs of man where applicable. She is his often his practice audience, his counselor, his truth advisor, his sounding board, his love interest, his chef, his taskmaster, and his ultimate teammate as he climbs the rungs of personal success. A good woman is so amazing because she does all the aforementioned often while putting her dreams on hold and never murmuring a sound of complaint. Does this not substantiate validity? I believe it does.

Another reason why a woman can't be considered invalid is the fact that 50% of the world's population are women. This is a major indicator of validity in that it confirms the fact that women comprise one half of the human population of this world. Similarly, the female population of the United States is currently at 51% which represents a majority. It is difficult to overlook or dispute the relevance of validated statistics. Since women comprise the majority of the United States population and half of the world population, I think it is safe to say that, based on economic, sociological, and political concerns, a woman can never be invalid.

Moreover, when and wherever the subject of love arises, it is almost inevitable that somewhere in the discussion a woman will somehow be involved, mentioned, discussed, or reflected upon. A chronological travel through history will afford one with countless notation of the beauty of a woman and how it related to love in some way. Love is a woman's special gift. It is a gift that heals, sooths, comforts, and thrills. When a woman loves a man and he loves her back, her touch becomes his need. When a woman loves a man and he loves her back, her presence becomes his dream. When a woman loves a man and he loves her back, her proximity becomes his extended extremity – solidifying oneness. Love is that intangible that binds hearts forevermore! Because love is love and love is that special gift that every woman has plenty of, A WOMAN CAN NEVER BE INVALID!

But hang on, if you were just about to think that love was the ultimate reason supporting the fact that a woman can never be invalid, read on? Of all the reasons why a woman can never be invalid, CHILDBIRTH is the single most significant reason alone. To put it plain, a woman exists as the sole vessel specifically designed to save humanity from extinction! Without a woman, humanity would face extinction. No human can be born without her. This is an undeniable truth. Without the woman, childbirth would be nonexistent! "Women are not perfect nor are men. But one thing I am certain of, a woman is completely and unmistakably VALID to this world! ...If you do not believe me, do some historical research: Look at family. Look at sacrifice. Look at female success. Look at male success. Look at history. Look at situations of love. Check tape! I rest my case!"

There is something I feel I must say to you dear Woman at this particular point of exploration. You are seeking attention today – and a lot of it. I have noticed that some of you are even seeking attention to get more attention than the next woman or young lady. Why is this so? Do you not realize your unique beauty? Do you not realize the fact that no one can beat you being the real you better than you – once you know you! You are the authority on YOU! You are the CEO of YOU! Be YOU in all the ways you choose to look and in all the things you choose to do! I suspect that some women and young ladies feel more confident of themselves when they receive any attention – whether good or bad. This in itself is unhealthy for personal growth.

I have also found that a lot of women and young ladies often struggle with peer pressure and the fear of social rejection for failing to dress like the popular trends regardless of how risque' the trends may become.

Dear Woman and young lady, find your you that is inside of you first, before attempting to dress and adorn the outside of you. Once you know your you, you can be fashionable being you in and around any trend! Your elegance becomes fashionable amongst any trend during any season! Don't lower your standards regarding the quality of respect you will allow for yourself. Don't lower your standards regarding the quality of respect you will accept from men – or anybody else. Don't lower your standards in terms of self-modesty. A Goddess pursues the objective of sleek and sweet modest sexiness, always! A Goddess exemplifies class, dignity, modest sensuality, confidence, kindness, beauty, and grace in everything that she does! "REAL MEN OF VALUE SHALL FIND HER ALWAYS!"

Let the imagination of the minds of men get needed exercise whenever they gaze upon your beauty. This will preserve enhancement of their individual and collective respect and appreciation of your total essence. Sleek and sweet modesty is key, not immodest physical exposure. You are too good to be perceived inappropriately.

THE PURPOSE

My purpose in writing this book is simply to encourage the essence of a woman. I sought to encourage intuitive thought to enhance personal strength, self-confidence, and optimism for her future. I also sought to allow the internal voice of my adoration for her to speak as poetic rivers of love upon her heart. I have benefited greatly from the many words, touches, experiences, and important lessons left upon my soul from the tenders of essence embedded in the love of said rivers. I sought to encourage the essence of a woman to love, be loved, and achieve better so that overall, she will become better at being the amazing Goddess that she already is. This has been an intriguing endeavor and I hope that you received value from reading this book and the wisdom of your heart has been broadened regarding the beauty, strength, wisdom, and true value of women to this world. In writing this book, my heart opened to speak truth always and always love.

This all began many years ago when I woke up inside of a dream desiring to explore this most wonderful of God's creations, the magnificent woman and her many special gifts and qualities. I am humbled by her awesomeness. I have found that true beauty has no mandated size, shape, weight, color, or creed. Beauty is just beauty. No one person on this planet has the right to determine whether a woman is physically beautiful or not. Once she was born, she awakened into instant beauty granted to her by the infinite love and design of God himself. SHE WAS BORN

BEAUTIFUL! But the world has chosen not to believe nor honor this truth. When viewing a woman, I find it important that every person realize the fact that BECAUSE HER APPEARANCE MAY NOT BE THE APPEARANCE OF YOUR CHOICE OR DOES NOT MEET YOUR PERSONAL PREFERENCES, DOES NOT DEEM HER TO BE UGLY AND UNDESIRABLE OR UNATTRACTIVE TO ALL. Moreover, anyone that says otherwise is either sadly mistaken or deliberately lying to the truth.

Woman, free yourself now of manipulation and gracefully flow into your real truth about you – in you, anxiously waiting for freedom and your voice! I remain ever impressed with how you, dear Goddess, have blessed this world with beauty, wisdom, compassion, strength, sacrifice, and hope. I believe that without you, we could never have imagined the start of nations, nor imagined the virgin thoughts of the concept of family. I believe that without you, there may never have been a perpetuation of families in and over history as the facts speak today.

Woman, oh woman, you are truly an amazing being for which the world should render honor, praise, and appreciation on all levels. For without you, man's desire for love would be left starving on its deaf bed. Woman, without you, man's inspiration for finding self-confidence would be extremely weakened. Woman, oh woman, without you, man's instinct of protection would be without real power and conviction. Woman, without you, man's ability to imagine and find true passion in his compassion would be - not to be.

Woman, oh woman, without you man's life-stand, which props him up and supports him, would be permanently broken. Your often silent and invisible presence behind and along-side of him would be no more. Woman, without you, children would seize to learn complete and unconditional love in its fullest form. Woman, oh woman, without you, sensuality would be without real tangibility within the minds of men. Woman, without you, we would be without our continuing possibility and potential for greatness as individual nations and as one world. I believe that it is the woman who weaves the fibers of family, community, and countries together and she effectively holds them together through her unique God-given gift of inspiring and sharing love. You see, man is very important to the same, but it is the woman that has nurtured and impacted every boy in some way prior to him becoming a man. It is a woman that gave every boy his life through God's magnificent process of childbirth. I believe that a good man is best suited to train a boy to become a good man. However, in the absence of a good man as in my case by the sudden death of my father, a good woman can get the job done. I am a living testimony.

Even human Goddesses experience pain. In life it is inevitable to experience two things. One is joy and the other is pain. Joy is easy, there usually is not mental effort required, and it is typically a very positive experience. Pain, on the other hand, is usually not easy and typically requires mental effort of some sort to cope with it. However, pain is nothing to be ashamed of. It is simply one of the body's early warning sensors. It is a true expression of emotion being triggered by physical or emotional stimulation. I know some of you today are struggling with confidence. Some of you are challenged with loneliness. Some of you are fighting victimization and you are smothered with humiliation. Some of you are paralyzed by jealousy and tormented by insecurity. Some of you even desire invisibility due to body-shaming. Some of you are emotionally muted by the fear of your fears. And some of you may even want to end your life to stop the deeply unwanted internal tears. Stop now!

You, yes you, are too valuable to ever think of removing yourself from this world! I believe this fact with all the soul in and of me! Without you, special lady, there will be left a huge gap in the person who last received your needed smile. A huge gap would be left in that person who last received your hug – wrapped tenderly with only your unique smile.

The way you walk. The way you talk. The way you look. That way you be you – will leave a huge gap in the hearts of those who know you least and those who know you more. Sweet lady of love, if you were to leave, you would leave an enormous gap in this world's deficient possibilities. This, Dear Love, again speaks of your true value and of yet other beautiful things that you, A Woman, can do!

I want you to know how valuable you are. I want you to know just how important you are to all life. Now, this moment, Kevin Rowe celebrates all of you! I want you to know you are important to my life. I love you.

Turn all of your pain into fuel for your immediate future gain! You are already unstoppable; you just have to realize it and GIVE YOURSELF PERMISSION TO BE IT! NOW - NOT LATER!

I've got good news for you! You can free yourself from these types of struggles and live the life you love. I want you to know that you shall never to be alone again from this point on because no matter what happens to you in the one life that you have, you will always have YOU! Your you is always with you! Make time to get to know this person well to learn everything that you can and cannot do in your one life! One other thing that you always have available to you is personal excellence – the ultimate level of self-improvement. Personal excellence will grant you the awesome ability to give excellence in every single thing that you do once you activate it in your life.

CHALLENGE YOUR CHALLENGE

For those of you who may not have a solution to effectively confront the various types of challenges mentioned above, I want to share a scaled down version of a problem-solving method I think may be of help to you:

When problems arise, it is important to remember not to panic. Stay calm. Panic will only lead to errors and bad decisions. I suggest that you utilize problem-solving techniques to effectively address your problems. I believe it is important to **IPIPF** (Identify; Prioritize; Isolate & Contain; Problem Solve; Follow-up).

- ❖ **I**-IDENTIFY: This is the first step of the process. You must first gather all of the facts then accept them.
- ❖ **P**-PRIORITIZE: This is the second step of the process. Now you must prioritize the threat(s) by level of severity. Rank them from greatest threat to smallest

threat. Once you know what you are dealing with, you can assess individual circumstances to prioritize effectively.

- ❖ **I**&C-ISOLATE & CONTAIN: This is the third step of the process. During this step, you begin by isolating the greatest threat posed from the lesser threats. Begin immediately placing the majority of your concentration on neutralizing the greatest threat. However, apply maintenance to all others.

- ❖ **PS**-PROBLEM SOLVING: This is the fourth step of the process. During the problem-solving phase, you must apply increased focus on solutions for the greatest threat immediately. You are to be constantly thinking of available resources to utilize and effectively initiate problem-solving efforts (i.e. applying appropriate solutions to the problem at hand). Activate necessary resources to the critical areas of the problem first. It is important that you continue deploying relevant and necessary resources to the problem until it has been contained and/or resolved. When appropriate or when the problem has been effectively neutralized, move on to the next greatest problem and implement the same process, respectively.

  *Remember to delegate lesser problems to other available qualified people and monitor their progress where applicable.

- ❖ **F**-FOLLOW UP: This is the last step of the process. During this phase, you are to continue to check on each incident or problem periodically to ensure effective maintenance and modify efforts accordingly.   I hope this helps!

I choose now to disrupt the thought of thoughts currently unspoken within the minds of the misguided about the value of a woman. Therefore, I ask you...Are a woman's feelings too minute to matter? Is a woman too emotionally weak to lead effectively? Is a woman too passive to ever have ambition? Is a woman too shallow in the mind to have a big dream? Is a woman too lazy and only seeks to find a man to be his leech? Is a woman too naïve and believes that her body is her best offering to achieve success and to find true love? Is a woman too expendable to be one exclusive love in someone's life? Is a woman too desperate to deserve and receive fidelity? Is a woman too stupid to understand inequality? Is a woman too damaged to respect self-respect? Is a woman too numb to realize she's still worth loving? Is a woman too flawed to deserve respect each and every day? Is a woman too ignorant to know her place in the human race?

Change your thoughts now if you dared to answer yes to any of the immediately preceding questions before this question I must ask now. Is a woman too much of anything to be the exact magnificence she undeniably is? She is much, much, more than an object or a perception heard that you see. Clarify your vision of her by making time to feel and learn her essence to give you her truth and your clarity. Think now for yourself of all that a woman is to your life and of all her value to this evolving idiomatic world. To you, dear woman, those beautiful eyes that you have that these words you now see, think now to yourself all the wonders that you are and of all that exist as your possibility.

I want you to know that you are appreciated. I want you to know that all of the positive things that you do have value. Don't ever stop being every ounce of who you are! Don't you ever stop being every ounce of who you are!! You are needed in this world more than the world may ever tell you. Don't stop caring about caring about caring about people and fairness for all. Don't stop being the light of desire that allows man to see what hope feels like. Dear lady don't stop being the legs of societal stability because your support is needed. You have proven to all that you are beautiful, you are smart, you are capable, you are strong, and you are love cleverly constructed and composed. It is you woman that holds the magical key of change deep within you. You must keep your internal fire burning with hope for you have the power and determination within you to do everything you decide to do. There are no limitations capable of holding back a truly determined woman! The only way limitations can hold you back is if you grant them permission to imprison your mind and your will. You must never allow this to happen!

I have seen your pain and I have felt it as well many times from the soul received from looking into your eyes. I have seen your tears. I have heard your cries from the day and from the night. Man shall love you eternally, while retaining many imperfections. We know not all empirical causes of our actions and reaction toward you. We too desire to be happy just as you and we also desire to have our happiness include you, Goddess of love. But I believe that we, as men, can be better in how we love you. I believe that we can be better in how we respect you. I believe that we can be better in how we cherish you. Dear Goddess of love, I believe that we can be better in how we support your dreams. I believe that we can be better in how we honor you. I believe that we can be better in how we shine our morals to ever impress you internally and indefinitely.

To the men of the world, I am compelled to say "We are men, and we are more than capable of improving anything that we desire to improve! The world's infirmities call out for our supreme excellence and for our enormous, unified strength of change now – not later! We must rid ourselves of self-centeredness and ultra-greed to secure peace by boldly honoring all inalienable rights of humans through the excellence of mastered brotherhood." I also say to all men under the sweet power of sincere words, "WE MUST BECOME BETTER NOW TO ALL WOMEN OF THIS WORLD AS BLISSFUL HARMONY IMPATIENTLY AWAITS THE ARRIVAL OF AMELIORATED MASCULINITY".

I believe convenience, in fact too much convenience, is literally sabotaging the character of people today. Rather than think for ourselves, we try to buy everything that is smart to do our thinking for us. We should never become unpracticed in thinking. People are now getting stuck on the tracks of social media and reality TV - unable to find the train stop of moderation while being blinded by the allure of unquenched mass approval. We now see nations missing the same train stops on their respective tracks. Is this a real phenomenon or simply false speculation? The answer lies in what you feel; what you feel after what you see; what you truly see after what your mind knows afterwards to be real. Is it all real?

Dear woman you have proven to this world over and over that you can survive and overcome almost any challenge. For this very reason you are now being summonsed to be more and to give more to you and to this society desperately in need.

Thank you, dear woman, for being the silent partner of all greatness! I celebrate you! You are 51% of the world's population! That says to the world that the potential of your united power is tremendous. You must use your power to help the people of this nation and this world to become better. This is my life's purpose and everything that I do must help people. I live inside of love each day. I seek to fulfill each second of each minute with love. I seek to fill every morsel of a minute of my queen's life with massive love. I do this by living each waking day as if I expire at 12 midnight. This allows me to focus on what really matters in my life each day. Try it and see if it yields you positive results? I BELIEVE IN THE GOODNESS IN EVERY PERSON! Everybody is Somebody! Everybody truly is Somebody! All human life has value! All human life is valuable! Why do we make it so hard to love one another when love itself was never meant to be difficult? Love, true love, was meant to be easy and free to give – not hard.

I urge you to rise in excellence and be a standard bearer of personal excellence! Be the standard bearer of civility! Be the standard bearer of internal beauty! You can do it! You are that needed mountain of determination! You are that needed reservoir of optimism! You are that ever-flowing stream of compassion! You are that needed pilar of joy! You are the needed eyes of unity! Woman, you are that needed storehouse of excellence! You are the needed hands of fairness! Dear Woman, you are that mighty river of peace! You are that needed basin of tranquility! You are that needed train of diversity! You are that needed tree of forgiveness! Dear Goddess, you are the needed silent partner of joy! You are the heart of beauty! Dear Goddess, you are that needed ambassador of love! GO FORTH AND UNLEASH YOUR GREATNESS! TAKE YOUR RIGHTFUL PLACE AND NEVER APOLOGIZE FOR YOUR AWESOMENESS! This world needs you WOMAN – Goddess of love and excellence.

I am encouraged today! I am proud to love women. I am proud to honor women! I am proud to have an amazing woman in my life. I am confident that we can, we must, and we will become better as a nation to respect and honor all women. I am also confident that we will become better and treat each other better by adopting personal excellence as a way of life. I am confident that we can begin to re-socialize the people of the world to refrain from inflicting psychological manipulations and negative socializations upon the women of the world. I believe these unwanted actions are direct results of diffused capitalism, self-centered impulses of greed and self-serving desires of troubled men and misguided women. This must stop! Now – not later!

We must do a better job of educating the people of America about American Values, fairness, real beauty, and real love. Equality should ever ring loudly and freely throughout this nation and throughout this world! You see, love has no size, height, weight, color, race, or creed. Love is simply love. All other things are simply add-ons to love. Think about little toddlers crawling around on the floor with other toddlers. They are unaware of size, height, weight, color, race, or creed and they play with and love each other unconditionally. We could learn a lot from the behavior of toddlers as it relates to cultivating unity and unconditional love. The point I would like to make is children love simply to love until they are taught to do otherwise. Let us use more of our freedom to share more love freely! As I have said before, I believe that we can always be better! This nation is in need of moral courage from its people. This nation and this world are both in need of excellence from its people and their leaders. The time is now for each of us to decide to become a better human now - not later!

Woman, oh woman, you are who you are and what you are to be to this world. Woman, oh woman, you are what you are and what you are supposed to be to me forever - PRECIOUS.

 Woman you were made to endure and not to fade. You were made to love in your own way and to be awesome every day. Woman, oh Woman, you were made this way because you can contend with the impossible!

Believe in yourself immensely and intensely! Embrace and love you and every single piece of what you are. Be the first to respect all of you in every way each and every day! Rise now with even more elegance, self-love, and confidence! Let us work together to become better to help this nation become better – to help this world heal and become better! BECAUSE WOMAN YOU CAN DO EVERYTHING YOUR HEART DREAMS POSSIBLE!

I love you Woman! Stay awesome! Stay beautiful! Stay you!!

"NOW, SOMEBODY PLEASE TELL ME EVERYTHING A WOMAN CAN'T DO?..."

ABOUT THE AUTHOR

Kevin Rowe

 Kevin Rowe understands the difference between saying you love a woman and actually, fully, and completely loving a woman. At the tender age of 7, after the sudden death of his father, he and his family began a new path of destiny heavily laced with poverty and struggle. Nevertheless, he learned to dream big with his eyes open. He learned the importance of studying, learning, and working to master himself. Kevin found personal excellence and made it a part of his personal DNA, a value, and the standard for his life.

Through personal excellence, he learned to persevere when others would quit. He learned to befriend the friendless when others believed they could not. He learned to help the helpless even when others said he should not. He learned to love the loveless when others simply would not. Kevin learned the awesome power of love and love became a part of him. He realized early that his purpose in life was to love, help, and protect people as he continues to do today. Kevin's life has afforded him a deep love and devotion to women because the eyes of his heart were opened early to see the great value and beauty of a woman's true essence and love.

For four decades, Kevin studied, applied, experienced, and examined the power of love as well as personal excellence in the laboratory of life. He discovered the amazing benefits that true love and personal excellence offer to the lives of people, and he has dedicated his life to sharing his wisdom and experience regarding both.

Kevin is a retired Division Commander. He is also a Motivational Keynote Speaker, Author, Entrepreneur, Personal Excellence expert, Human Relations Strategist, Mindset Surgeon, and a Leadership and Performance Consultant. Kevin is an advocate for woman and for human excellence. He lives inside of love each second of each moment of each day! He believe in the good in every human. He is on a mission to help people become better. Now - not later!

BOOKS BY THIS AUTHOR

The Pursuit Of Personal Excellence

The Pursuit of Personal Excellence (the POPE) is an exhilarating introspective journey of disciplined mental mastery. The POPE gives you the solution for positive change to fulfill your dreams! It will equip you with the tools necessary to change your life from mediocre to phenomenal! The POPE will help you transform your life with mental discipline and a personal commitment to excellence sprinkled with love, compassion, integrity, self-knowledge, confidence, and personal mental power!
If youre looking for personal power and purpose in your life, the POPE is your answer!
Rich or poor, the POPE will inspire you!
The POPE dares to change the world!

www.ingramcontent.com/pod-product-compliance
Lightning Source LLC
Chambersburg PA
CBHW070051260726
48658CB00002B/847